Duh

...and other observations by TOLES

Andrews and McMeel
A Universal Press Syndicate Company
Kansas City

Tom Toles is distributed internationally by Universal Press Syndicate.

Duh copyright © 1996 by Buffalo News. All rights reserved. Printed in the United States of America. No part of this book may be used or reproduced in any manner whatsoever without written permission except in the case of reprints in the context of reviews. For information write Andrews and McMeel, a Universal Press Syndicate Company, 4520 Main Street, Kansas City, Missouri 64111.

ISBN: 0-8362-1088-3

Library of Congress Catalog Card Number: 95-81470

For Gretchen

November 1, 1992

November 6, 1992

January 13, 1993

February 10, 1993

The Arkansas Chainsaw Massacre

March 16, 1993

Timber Co. official explaining how a second-growth tree farm can be as majestic in its way as an ancient old-growth forest.

EITHER THAT OR HE'S WAVING TO THE IMAGINARY SPECIES WHO LIVE THERE.

March 30, 1993

April 9, 1993

April 11, 1993

April 15, 1993

Round and round and round he goes.

May 14, 1993

May 27, 1993

May 28, 1993

The Sequel

June 6, 1993

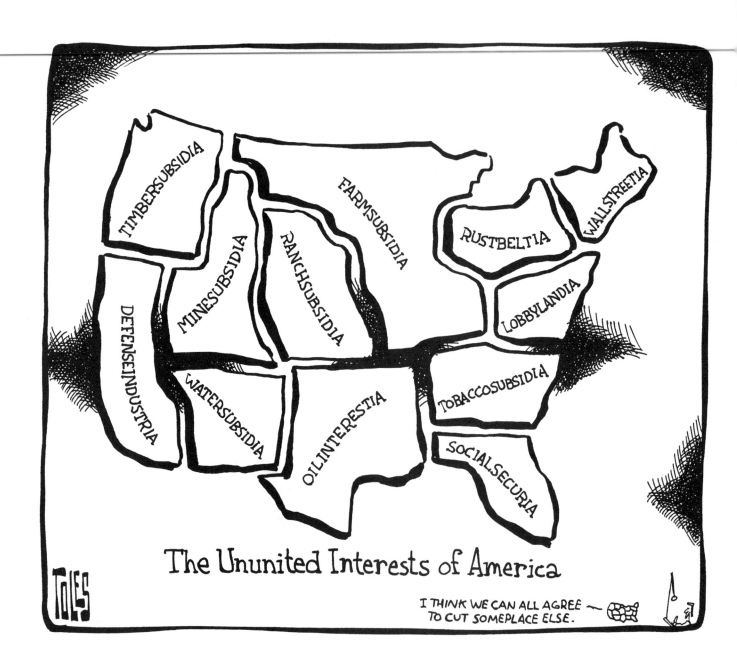

June 16, 1993

July 1, 1993

July 4, 1993

22

August 16, 1993

September 28, 1993

November 24, 1993

25

December 6, 1993

December 23, 1993

January 12, 1994

If Detroit cars worked the way Detroit works.

YOU'D NEED A LOBBYIST TO SELL THEM.

February 4, 1994

February 9, 1994

30

The proposed Disney American History Theme Park 'would be split into nine "playlands" with themes that include slavery in America and the wrenching era of the Vietnam War.' —N.Y. Times

I LOVED HEARING MICKEY READ THE EMANCIPATION PROCLAMATION IN HIS FUNNY LITTLE VOICE.

TOLES

February 28, 1994

31

March 29, 1994

Richard M. Nixon

37ᵀᴴ PRESIDENT OF THE U.S.

Architect of detente with the Soviet Union and the opening to China. Served as congressman, senator, vice president under Eisenhower and elected president in 1968. But in his reelection

resigned. Continued in public life to earn status as political elder statesman.

TOLES

18½ MINUTE GAP

HE WAS A...

...PRESIDENT.

April 26, 1994

May 4, 1994

May 13, 1994

May 18, 1994

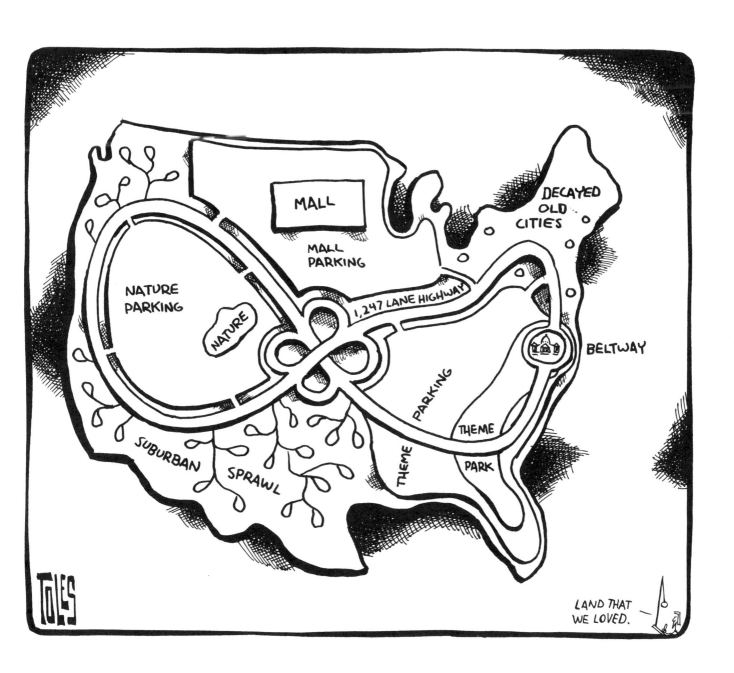

June 3, 1994

June 9, 1994

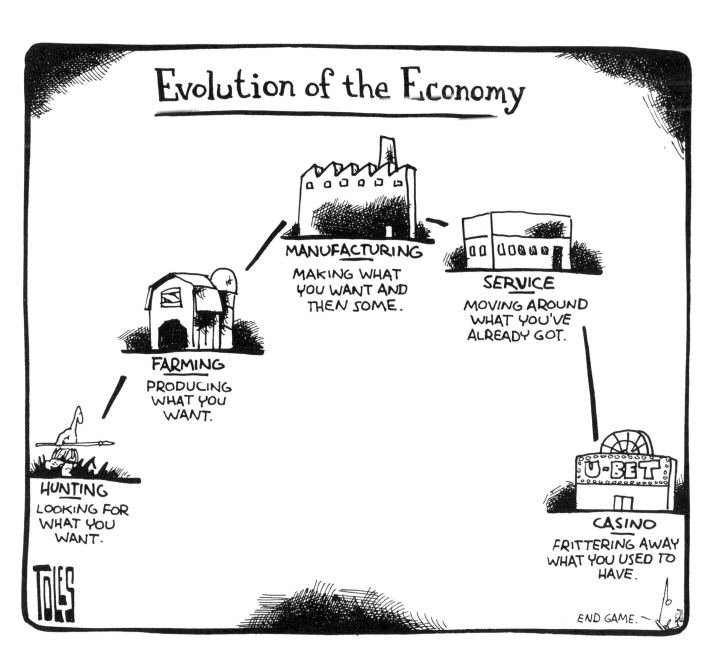

Evolution of the Economy

HUNTING
LOOKING FOR WHAT YOU WANT.

FARMING
PRODUCING WHAT YOU WANT.

MANUFACTURING
MAKING WHAT YOU WANT AND THEN SOME.

SERVICE
MOVING AROUND WHAT YOU'VE ALREADY GOT.

CASINO
FRITTERING AWAY WHAT YOU USED TO HAVE.

END GAME.

TOLES

July 14, 1994

July 15, 1994

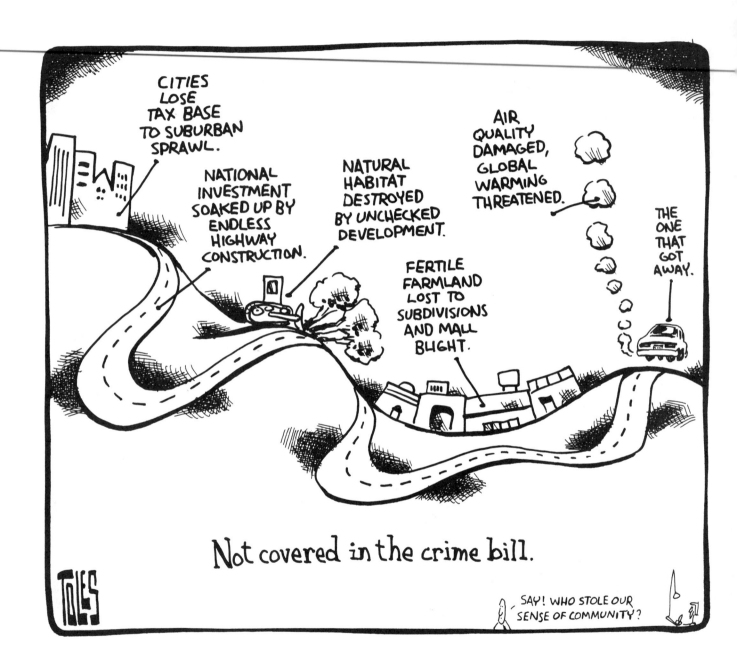

August 4, 1994

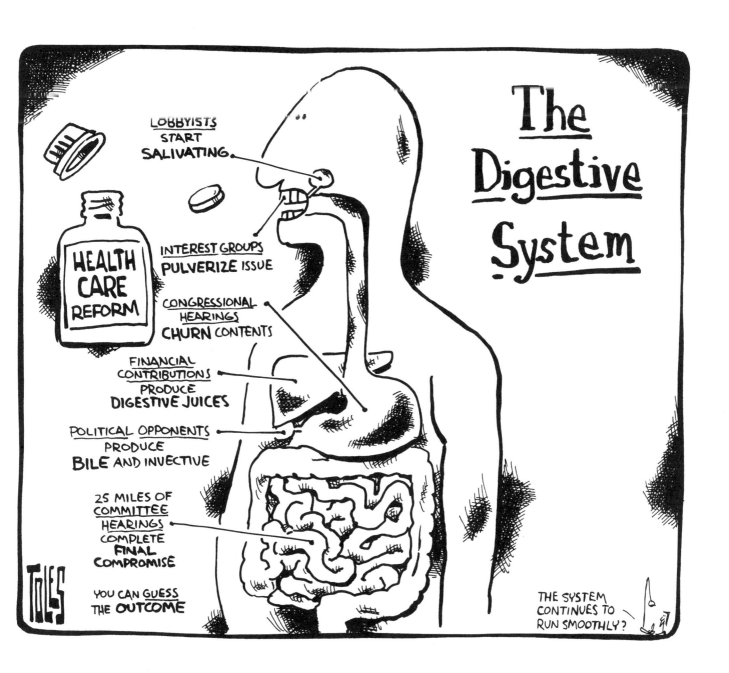

August 5, 1994

43

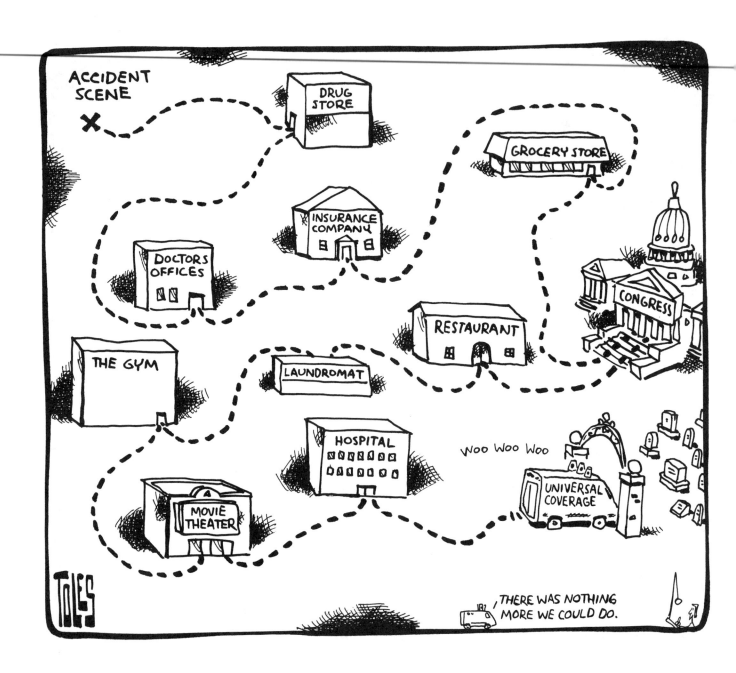

September 4, 1994

September 8, 1994

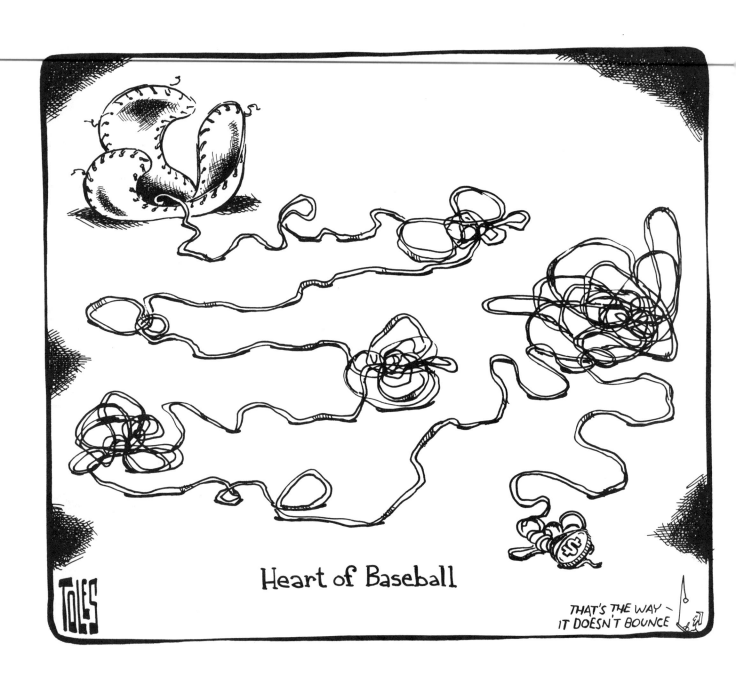

Heart of Baseball

TOLES

THAT'S THE WAY —
IT DOESN'T BOUNCE

September 18, 1994

The threat of inflation

September 21, 1994

September 28, 1994

September 30, 1994

49

Simpson Juror Questionnaire

Are you easily swayed by press reports?

Yes.

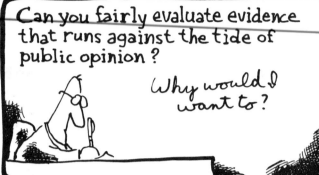

Can you fairly evaluate evidence that runs against the tide of public opinion?

Why would I want to?

Have you ever been tempted to slit an enemy's throat?

Lots of times.

How would you feel about a deadlocked jury?

Fine with me.

If you were the last vote needed for a verdict, how would you handle it?

Hold out for more money.

TOLES

YOU'RE NOT QUALIFIED FOR JURY DUTY, BUT HAVE YOU CONSIDERED RUNNING FOR CONGRESS?

THE BILL CLINTON JURY?

October 4, 1994

October 16, 1994

October 25, 1994

November 1, 1994

The Gingrinch who stole Christmas

November 21, 1994

November 27, 1994

December 31, 1994

January 3, 1995

January 8, 1995

January 17, 1995

January 25, 1995

January 30, 1995

February 17, 1995

February 23, 1995

February 24, 1995

February 26, 1995

65

February 26, 1995

March 3, 1995

March 6, 1995

March 7, 1995

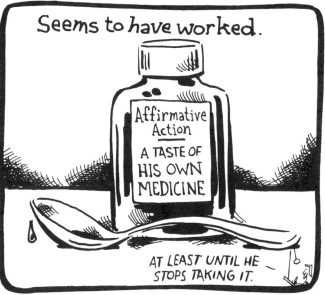

March 8, 1995

March 26, 1995

April 2, 1995

April 4, 1995

THE VIETNAMIZATION OF THE WAR ON POVERTY. —

April 7, 1995

April 19, 1995

April 21, 1995

April 28, 1995

The 'Pain and Suffering Award' Debate

May 7, 1995

May 11, 1995

May 12, 1995

May 17, 1995

May 19, 1995

May 28, 1995

June 6, 1995

June 14, 1995

June 21, 1995

June 22, 1995

Welfare Cadillac, 1995

June 27, 1995

June 28, 1995

June 30, 1995

July 12, 1995

July 18, 1995

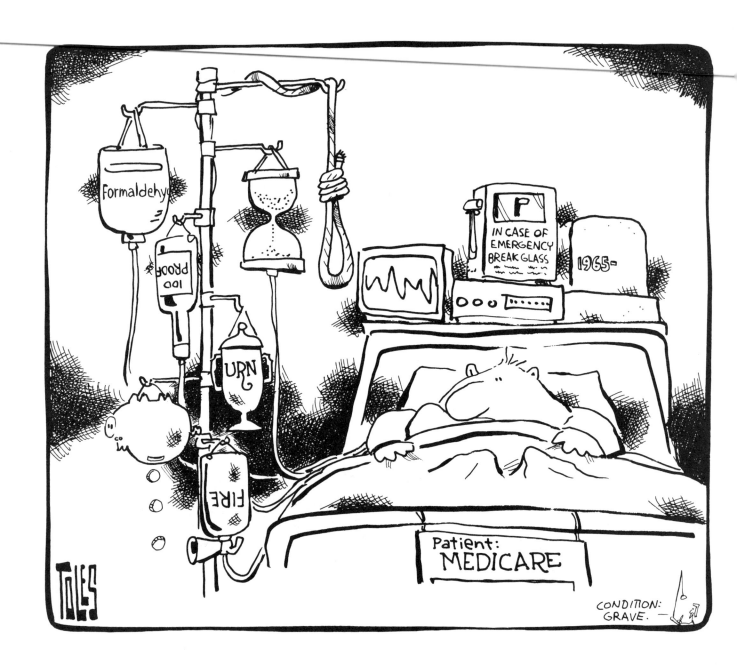

July 30, 1995

Sistine Chapel- NEA fund-cut version

TOLES

Sistine Chapel- NEA taste guidelines version

...BUT THEY KNOW WHAT THEY LIKE.

August 21, 1995

August 25, 1995

August 27, 1995

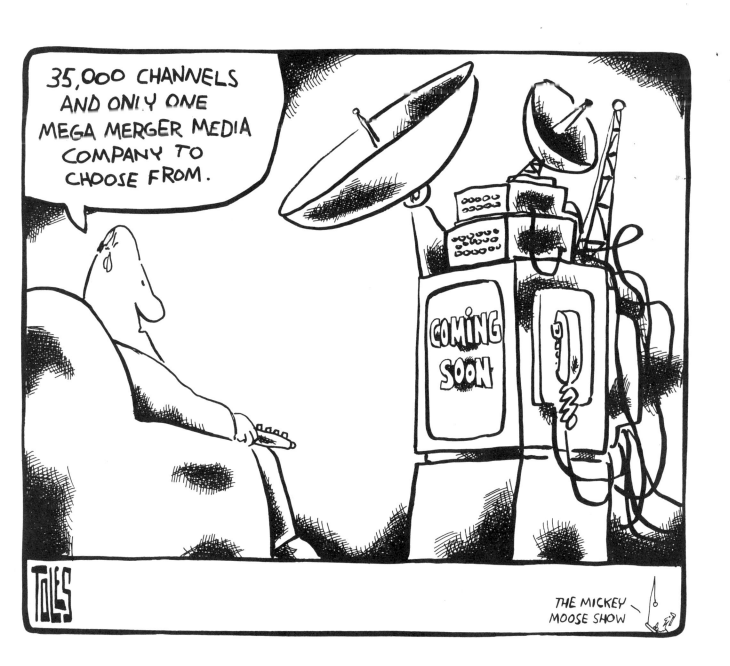

August 31, 1995

September 1, 1995

September 3, 1995

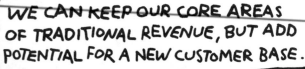

September 6, 1995

Bob Dole's drive to make Pandering our official language.

September 7, 1995

September 12, 1995

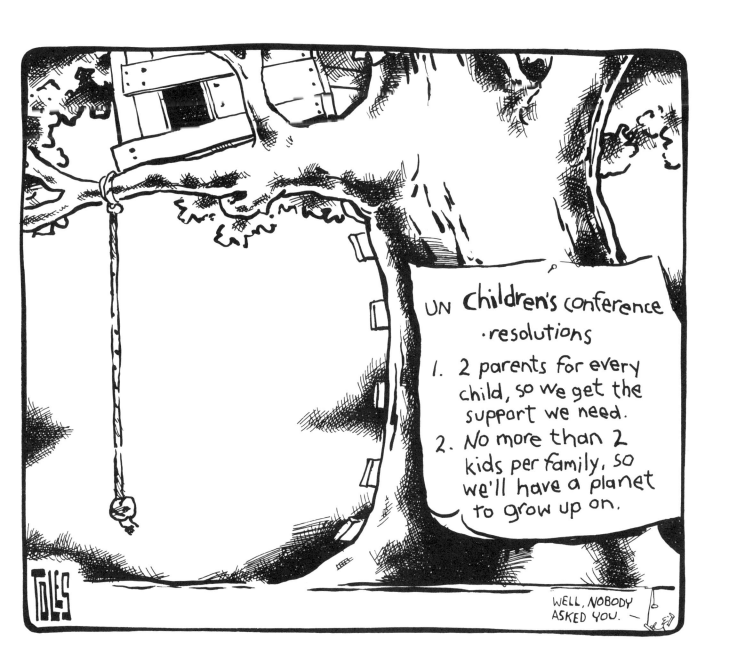

September 18, 1995

September 21, 1995

September 26, 1995

September 29, 1995

Epidemic childhood obesity baffles researchers.

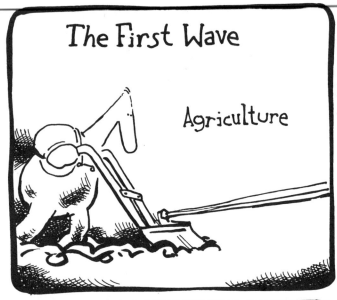

October 6, 1995

110

October 17, 1995

October 19, 1995

October 20, 1995

Smokers of distinction are learning what the great chefs have known for centuries.

When it comes to <u>flavor</u>, nothing beats <u>ammonia</u>.

Yes, tobacco companies now allow you too to savor the unbeatable taste of ammonia, long recognized as one of nature's most enchanting flavors.

Smoke it today. Ammonia. For flavor.

•<u>NOT</u> added to enhance nicotine delivery.

KIDS, <u>DON'T</u> TRY THIS AT HOME. —

October 22, 1995

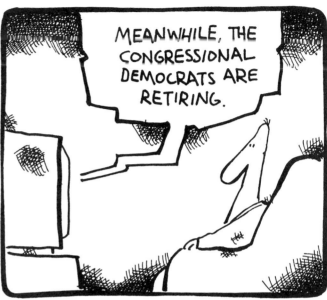

October 24, 1995

October 29, 1995

October 30, 1995

November 2, 1995

November 7, 1995

November 10, 1995

American Revolution II

FIRST IN THE HEART OF
HIS CONTRIBUTORS.

November 13, 1995

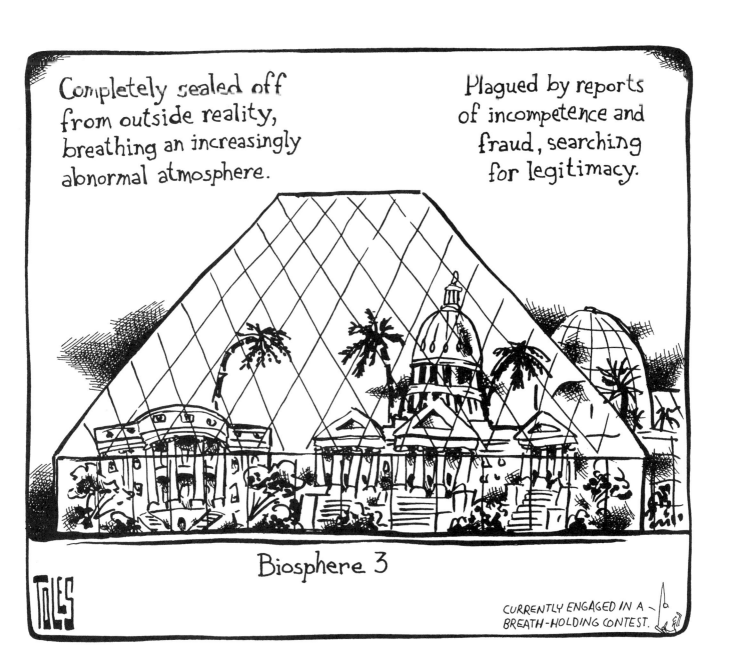

Completely sealed off from outside reality, breathing an increasingly abnormal atmosphere.

Plagued by reports of incompetence and fraud, searching for legitimacy.

Biosphere 3

TOLES

CURRENTLY ENGAGED IN A — BREATH-HOLDING CONTEST.

November 14, 1995

God's Junk Mail

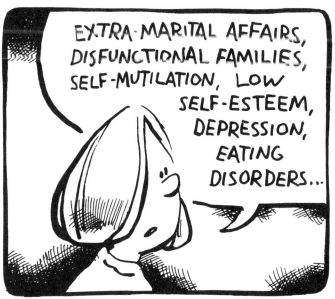

November 26, 1995

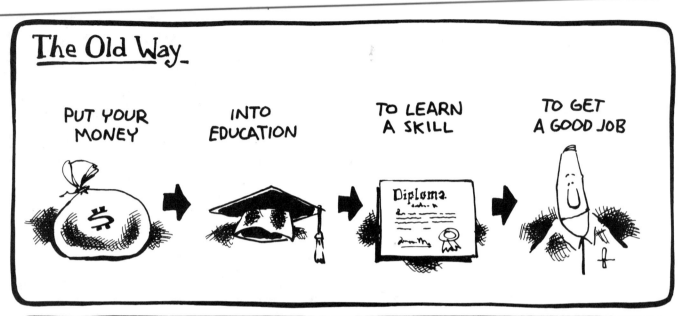

The Old Way.

PUT YOUR MONEY → INTO EDUCATION → TO LEARN A SKILL → TO GET A GOOD JOB

The New Way.

PUT YOUR MONEY → DIRECTLY INTO THE STOCK MARKET → FOR BIGGER RETURNS THAN ACTUALLY WORKING → AND THE ABILITY TO DEMAND THAT THEY DOWNSIZE THAT OTHER GUY'S GOOD JOB RIGHT OUT OF EXISTENCE.

STARTING HINT: INHERIT THE MONEY

TOLES

November 29, 1995

November 30, 1995

December 3, 1995